Kid's Bible Day-by-Day

365 Promises
from the Old & New Testament

Claudia Vurnakes

Published by Playmore, Inc. Publishers and Waldman Publishing Corp., New York, New York

Copyright © MM Playmore, Inc. Publishers and
Waldman Publishing Corp., New York, New York

Printed in Canada

1. Hath God said, and shall he not do it? or hath he spoken, and shall he not make it good?

—Numbers 23:19

2. Thy word is true from the beginning; and every one of thy righteous judgments endureth for ever.

—Psalm 119:160

3. For the promise is unto you, and to your children...

—Acts 2:39

The Bible is full of wonderful promises that God makes to you and to everyone who loves Him. How do you get these promises? First, know what God says, and believe it in your heart. Then, start living out each promise. God is faithful. He will always keep His word to you.

4. Fear thou not, for I am with thee: be not dismayed; for I am thy God: I will strengthen thee; yea, I will help thee.

—Isaiah 41:10

5. I will never leave thee, nor forsake thee.

—Hebrews 13:5

Friends move. Our favorite teacher leaves. Grandparents get old and die. Every time we turn around, it seems, someone special is going away, leaving our lives for good. The person who is left behind can feel scared and lonely. But there is Someone who always stays, Someone who is right by our side in good times and in bad. We have His Word on it!

6. Sing unto the Lord with thanksgiving;...who covereth the heaven with clouds, who prepareth rain for the earth, who maketh grass to grow upon the mountains.

—Psalms 147:8

7. While the earth remaineth, seedtime and harvest, and cold and heat, and summer and winter, and day and night shall not cease.

—Genesis 8:22

What if the sun simply stopped working, or the soil no longer grew any vegetables? What if winter stayed all year, all over the world? Long ago, the Lord promised that He would keep the earth running in a regular, orderly manner. God has been keeping that promise ever since. Even when terrible storms interrupt the cycle, we can look forward to the return of normal weather, because of this good promise.

8. My son, hear the instruction of thy father, and forsake not the law of thy mother: For they shall be an ornament of grace unto thy head, and chains about thy neck.

—Proverbs 1:8-9

9. Children, obey your parents in all things: for this is well pleasing unto the Lord.

—Colossians 3:20

10. Children, obey your parents in the Lord: for this is right. Honor thy father

and mother; which is the first commandment with promise. That it may be well with thee, and thou mayest live long on the earth.

—Ephesians 6:1-3

There is a big difference between obeying our parents and obeying them in the Lord. There is also a big difference between obey-

ing and honoring. These verses teach us that we are to go the extra mile in respecting our parents and cooperating with them. Use a washable marker and write the letter H on your hand. Every time you look down today, the H will remind you to honor your parents, with your actions and with your attitude.

God promises that when we obey this commandment, He will give us lives that are long and good. Living long enough to grow old and wise is a great blessing. It all starts with something very simple: obeying your mom and dad.

11. In my Father's house are many mansions; if it were not so, I would have told you. I go to prepare a place for you.

—**St. John 14:2**

A mansion is a big fancy house. There are many rooms in a mansion, each one filled

with the finest things that money can buy.
Would you like to live in a mansion? Some
day, you can! Jesus says that going to
Heaven will be like living in God's mansion,
and best of all, you won't need any money to
stay there. What you will need is true faith.
Jesus promises that He is at work right now,
making a wonderful home in Heaven for all
those who love and believe in Him.

12. But they that wait upon the Lord
shall renew their strength; they shall
mount up with wings as eagles. They
shall run, and not be weary; and they
shall walk, and not faint.

—Isaiah 40:31

Think how much fun it would be to soar
above the clouds like a mighty eagle, to fly

and fly, and never get tired! When do you need to be as strong as an eagle? Maybe you have a difficult chore to do, or your homework seems endless. Maybe a family problem is wearing you out. Ask God for help. He promises His strength and energy to all who put their faith in Him. Before you know it, you will find yourself soaring!

13. The blood of Jesus Christ his Son cleanseth us from all sin.

—I John 1:7

14. Behold the Lamb of God, which taketh away the sin of the world.

—St. John 1:29

15. He was wounded for our transgressions, he was bruised for our iniquities: the chastisement of our peace was upon him; and with his stripes we are healed.

—Isaiah 53:5

16. Neither by the blood of goats and calves, but by his own blood he entered in once into the holy place, having obtained eternal redemption for us.

—Hebrews 9:12

Sin is disobeying God. Our sins always hurt someone, and sooner or later, we feel horrible about them. We realize we have to do something to get rid of sin. All through the Old Testament, people sacrificed animals to pay for their sin. They had to do this over and over again, each time they sinned. But when Jesus died on the cross, His blood was so perfect and so powerful, no more sacrifices were required for any sin, anywhere.

You have God's promise: the penalty for your sin has already been paid—by Jesus!

17. I am fearfully and wonderfully made...

—**Psalm 139:14**

18. For the Lord seeth not as a man seeth; for man looketh on the outward appearance, but the Lord looketh on the heart.

—**1 Samuel 16:7**

So, you don't look like a top fashion model. You may not have the body of a champion athlete. God made you, and He knows your heart. He likes you, just the way you are. Each morning, when you look in the mirror, repeat these promises. Ask God to help you be the wonderful person He created, on the inside and on the outside. Soon, you will see yourself through God's eyes, and so will other people!

19. A wholesome tongue is a tree of life.

—Proverbs 15:4

20. Pleasant words are as an honey-comb: sweet to the soul, and health to the bones.

—Proverbs 16:24

21. Who so keepeth his mouth and his tongue keepeth his soul from troubles.

—Proverbs 21:23

The Bible has much to say about how we use our mouths. True, kind words bring life and health and peace—for ourselves and for others. Make sure that what comes from your mouth is good, so you can claim these promises!

22. If my people, which are called by my name, shall humble themselves, and pray, and seek my face, and turn from their wicked ways; then will I hear from

heaven, and will forgive their sin, and will heal their land.

—**2 Chronicles 7:14**

It is easy to get worried when you read the newspaper. Every day, there are stories about war and hatred and crime. How can the world be a good place in which to live, when evil things happen so often?

This promise reminds us that God is the one in charge. Only He can solve these problems. When we ask for His help, He will listen, and will heal our land from the disease of evil.

23. Trust in the Lord with all thine heart; and lean not unto thine own under
standing. In all thy ways acknowledge him, and he shall direct thy paths.

—**Proverbs 3:5-6**

Watch out! When you lean on your own ideas, it is easy to fall flat on your face. Try leaning on God. He will never let you down!

The Lord promises to show you the way when you put your faith in Him. In everything you do, turn to Him. He will make sure you are heading in the right direction and give you success.

24. The Lord is slow to anger.

—Nahum 1:3

25. Vengeance belongeth unto me, I will recompense, saith the Lord. And again, The Lord shall judge his people.

—Hebrews 10:30

26. Thou preparest a table before me in the presence of mine enemies:....my cup runneth over.

—Psalm 23:5

God loves us, and He gets angry when sin keeps us apart from Him. But His anger grows slowly. He gives us time to turn away from sin and come back to Him.

God also promises to deal with our enemies. He is angry when others hurt us. But we do not have to worry about handing out punishment. God Himself will see to that for us. In fact, He promises to bless us right before our enemies' eyes. What could be better than feasting on God's good blessings while the enemy watches in amazement?

27. Eye hath not seen, nor ear heard, neither have entered into the heart of man, the things which God hath prepared for them that love him.

1 Corinthians 2:9

Imagine that for one day, you could do anything, go anywhere your heart desired. What a great day that would be! But there is wonderful news! Days even better than that await every person who loves God. We cannot begin to imagine what He has in store for us, now in our life on this earth, and later on in Heaven. So if you are a believer, buckle your seat belt. There's a roller coaster ride straight ahead!

28. Thy word is a lamp unto my feet, and a light unto my path.

—Psalm 119:105

29. For the word of God is quick, and powerful, and sharper than any two-edged sword.

—Hebrews 4:12

God loves us so much, He gives us His very own words. The Bible is like the flashlight we carry when we walk in the dark. It lights the bumps and corners that could trip us up. Scripture also cuts deep into our hearts. It shows how far we are from being what God wants. Would you like to know God better? Read what He has written for you—in the Bible!

30. Peace I leave with you, my peace I give unto you.

—St. John 14:27

31. And he shall judge among the nations, and shall rebuke many peo-ple: and they shall beat their swords into plowshares, and their spears into pruning hooks: nation shall not lift up sword against nation, neither shall they learn war any more.

—Isaiah 2:4

32. Blessed are the peacemakers: for they shall be called the children of God.

—St. Matthew 5:9

Jesus knew all about hectic days. Everywhere He went, He caused a commotion. But through it all, Jesus had peace of mind. He did not fret or worry. Jesus promised His followers they could have this peace, too. It came from knowing that God was in control, and that everything would go accordir

Some day, the nations of the world will experience this same peace. There will be no more war because everyone will know and love Jesus. What a great day that will be! In the meantime, we are to work at bringing peace to people. Then God will call us His very own.

33. I will both lay me down in peace, and sleep: for thou, Lord, only makest me dwell in safety.

—Psalm 4:8

34. He giveth his beloved sleep.

—Psalm 127:2

35. He that keepeth thee shall not slumber.

—Psalm 121:3

God promises that He will never go to sleep on the job. He keeps watch over us all day and all night, so we can rest in peace. Sleep is one of God's best gifts. Remember this the next time you want to complain about your bedtime!

36. I will not leave you comfortless: I will come to you.

—**St. John 14:18**

37. Blessed are they that mourn: for they shall be comforted.

—**St. Matthew 5:4**

Most tears eventually stop. We cheer up and get on with life. But some sorrows just will not go away: the death of a loved one, a handicap, the diagnosis of a terrible disease. There is no medicine strong enough to cure a heart that is permanently broken. God can do what no one else can. He will hold you close and ease your pain. Do you have a broken heart? Tell Him about it today.

38. Behold, I make all things new.

Revelation 21:5

39. Thou shalt be called by a new name, which the mouth of the Lord shall name.

—Isaiah 62:2

Do you ever wish you could just start over? With God, you can! He promises a new beginning for every person who comes to Him. He forgives the sin in our past and wipes it away, as if it never existed.

Then He gives us a new, better way of living—through His power and strength.

40. If any of you lack wisdom, let him ask of God, that giveth to all men liberally.

—James 1:5

41. They that seek the Lord understand all things.

—Proverbs 28:5

King Solomon put God to the test with this promise. Instead of asking for wealth or power, he prayed to the Lord for wisdom. God was so pleased, He granted Solomon's request. Soon people from all over the world came to hear the king's wise advice. The next time you need wisdom, ask God!

42. Weeping may endure for a night, but joy cometh in the morning.

—Psalm 30:5

43. There shall be no more death, neither sorrow, nor crying, neither shall there be any more pain.

—Revelation 21:4

Sad days can seem endless, but the Bible promises that for each of us, a morning will come when we wake up happy again. We also have the promise of happiness that knows no end—in heaven. How wonderful it will be to live without death or tears or pain forever!

44. The gift of God is eternal life through Jesus Christ our Lord.

—Romans 6:23

45. Verily, verily, I say unto you, He that believeth on me hath everlasting life.

—St. John 6:47

Think of a piece of string that could reach from the earth to the sun. How long would it need to be? Eternal life is much, much longer. God loves us so much, He wants us to be with Him forever. It is good to know that when we believe in Jesus, our life will never, ever end.

46. I can do all things through Christ which strengthen me.

—Philippians 4:13

47. If God be for us, who can be against us?

—**Romans 8:31**

"M-m-me? Give a speech in front of the whole school?"

"I'll never get those bullies to back off! It's six against one!"

The next time you face a tough challenge, remember Jesus. If He was strong enough to overcome death on the cross, He is strong enough to handle your situation. His power flows through you, and God is on your side.

48. For I am the Lord, I change not.

—**Malachi 3:6**

49. With whom is no variableness, neither shadow of turning.

—**James 1:17**

Have you ever had a friend who changed and then stopped being your friend? It is hard to accept the fact that people do not always stay the same. But God is the same, yesterday, today and tomorrow. He will never change. He will always be your friend.

50. Being fully persuaded that what he had promised, he was able also to perform.

—Romans 4:21

51. He is faithful that promised.

—Hebrews 10:23

We hear promises everywhere: from our family, from our friends, from television commercials. For many of us, promises are easy to make, and even easier to break. But God is the Great Promise-Keeper. When He gives us His word, He will do exactly what He says, at just the right time. No matter what, we can count on Him!

52. Our sufficiency is of God.

—2 Corinthians 3:5

53. My grace is sufficient for thee: for my strength is made perfect in weakness.

—2 Corinthians 12:9

Sufficient means having enough. When we have God in our hearts, we have enough for anything that comes along in our lives. We discover we have enough of God's power to be strong in hard times. We have enough of His love to overcome hatred. We miraculously find enough time and energy to do His work. On our own, we will never have what it takes. But when we have God, we have enough.

54. Them that honor me, I will honor.

—1 Samuel 2:30

55. If any man serve me, him will my Father honor.

—St. John 12:26

Eric Liddell was a great runner who went to the Olympics. When he got there, he learned that his race was set for Sunday, the Lord's Day. Instead of running to win the gold medal, Eric went to church. Many people thought he had thrown away the chance of a lifetime. But God honored the young athlete who honored Him. Three days later, Eric got to run in another race and set a new Olympic record.

56. Honor the Lord with thy substance, and with the first fruits of all thine increase: So shall thy barns be filled with plenty.

—Proverbs 3:9-10

57. He that giveth unto the poor shall not lack.

—Proverbs 28:27

Money is hard to earn, and most of us want to hold on to every last penny. But God makes a very curious promise about money. "Share it with others," He says. "Then you will always have what you need." When we give our offerings to God, He promises to pour out His blessings on us. Try it! Give to God, then watch to see what He gives back to you.

58. The kingdom of God is. . .right-eousness, and peace, and joy.

—Romans 14:17

59. He hath put a new song in my mouth.

—Psalm 40:3

Joy is finding delight in everyday life. It is

having fun with your pesky younger brother, or being happy about a beautiful sunset, or

feeling so good you could sing. Joy is a sign that God lives in your heart. The next time you feel joyful, remember that He is at work in your life, and thank Him.

60. I am the Lord your God, and none else: and my people shall never be ashamed.

—Joel 2:27

61. For I am not ashamed of the gospel

of Christ: for it is the power of God unto salvation to every one that believeth.

—Romans 1:16

Are you embarrassed about loving God? Do you keep your faith a secret from friends at school? The Lord promises that we will never have a reason to be ashamed of Him. People may laugh about God now, but some day they will know the truth, when He gives eternal life to all who love and believe in Him.

62. He shall call upon me, and I will answer him.

—Psalm 91:15

63. Before they call, I will answer; and while they are yet speaking, I will hear.

—Isaiah 65:24

You never get a busy signal when you call on God. He is always ready to listen. Talk to God the way you would to a friend you really respect. Tell Him all your thoughts, not just the nice ones. He loves to hear praise and thanksgiving, but He pays attention to sad or angry prayers, too. Even before you finish speaking, God will understand.

64. If ye...know how to give good gifts unto your children, how much more shall your Father, which is in heaven, give good things to them that ask him?

—St. Matthew 7:11

65. The Spirit itself maketh intercession for us.

—Romans 8:26

Sometimes a problem is so complicated, we don't know how to pray about it. Don't worry.

The Bible says that the Holy Spirit takes each prayer that is prayed and makes it right, and then places it before God. Just keep on praying, and know that God will give you the answer that is always best and right.

66. He is a rewarder of them that dili-

gently seek him.

—Hebrews 11:6

67. Seek, and ye shall find.

—St. Matthew 7:7

One of the first Russian astronauts said that he looked for God when he flew into space, but did not find Him. That was his way of saying there was no God. We know better. If that astronaut had truly looked for God with his whole heart, he would have found Him—not out in space, but working in his life, blessing him and helping him understand.

Behold... The Lord

68. For we are his workmanship.

—**Ephesians 2:10**

69. He which hath begun a good work in you will perform it until the day of Jesus Christ.

—**Philippians 1:6**

Have you ever watched a skilled craftsman work? He takes such care with every detail, to make sure the finished product will be perfect. That's how God feels about you. You are his good work, and He will not stop working on you until you are just right. Remember this when you don't feel very good about yourself. God is not finished yet.

70. For mine house shall be called a house of prayer for all people.

—Isaiah 56:7

71. In thee shall all nations be blessed.

—Galatians 3:8

God thinks big. He is very happy when one person comes to love Him. But He will be the happiest when everyone, all over the world, has heard about Him. His blessings are for all people everywhere. You can help by making sure all kinds of people feel welcome when they come to your church.

72. Take unto you the whole armour of God, that ye may be able to withstand in the evil day.

—Ephesians 6:13

73. The Lord is my strength and my shield.

—Psalm 28:7

Wouldn't it be great to have an invisible suit of armor that would protect you from others' hurtful words? You do! God promises that He is the shield between you and your enemy. The insults will bounce off and not hurt, because God's love and His truth protect you.

74. Ye shall know the truth, and the truth shall make you free.

—St. John 8:32

75. Let thy loving kindness and thy truth continually preserve me.

—Psalm 40:11

Do you want to know what is true, and real, and right? God promises that His Word is truth. Many other words sound true today: commercials, the lyrics to popular songs, even things famous people say. But most of those words will not be around tomorrow. Only God's true Word can free us forever from sin and wrong thinking.

76. As newborn babes, desire the sincere milk of the word, that ye may grow thereby.

—1 Peter 2:2

77. O taste and see that the Lord is good.

—Psalm 34:8

Little babies just love to eat! No one has to teach them how. They are born craving milk. And when they eat, they grow big and strong. That will happen to us when we learn to crave God's Word, to "eat" it every day. God promises it will even taste good. Try it. You'll like it!

78. The Lord is my shepherd.
—**Psalm 23:1**

79. We are his people, the sheep of his pasture.
—**Psalm 100:3**

80. Behold, I, even I, will both search my sheep, and seek them out.
—**Ezekiel 34:11**

81. He shall feed his flock like a shepherd: he shall gather the lambs with his arm.
—**Isaiah 40:11**

God loves you just like a shepherd loves his littlest lamb! Sheep need plenty of attention. The shepherd must help them find grass and fresh water. He must protect them from danger, and care for them when they are sick or hurt. A good shepherd will even search all night for a lamb who has wandered away from the flock.

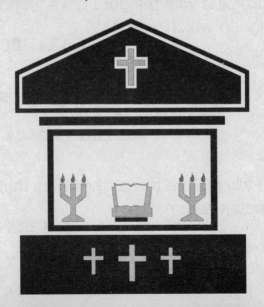

It is good to know that we are God's lambs. No matter where we go, He will come looking for us, to bring us to greener pastures.

82. I will seek that which was lost.
Ezekiel 34:16

83. Rejoice with me; for I have found my sheep which was lost.
—St. Luke 15:10

84. Let us eat, and be merry: for this my son. . was lost, and is found.
—St. Luke 15: 23-24

85. I will restore to you the years that the locust hath eaten.
—Joel 2:25

Jesus is the Seeker, the Finder, the Savior. No one and no thing can stay lost in Him. Maybe you have lost hope, or you can't find anything to be happy about. Maybe you have taken a wrong turn and lost your way in life. Jesus promises to find you.

Even wasted time is not lost when you trust God. Long ago, the people disobeyed God and enemy armies came and destroyed their crops for several years in a row. But God kept His promise. He reached out and found his people's hearts, and repaid them for the harvests that had been lost with good weather and bumper crops. He will do the same for you. Turn to Him whenever you feel lost.

86. To everything there is a season, and a time to every purpose under the heaven.

—Ecclesiastes 3:1

87. My times are in thy hand.
—**Psalm 31:15**

Rush, wait, rush, wait! Many of us have trouble managing our time. But God promises that He is the One in control of our time. He knows just the right time for our birth and our death, and for everything in between. Things happen when He plans them, at the perfect time.

88. Know ye not that your body is the temple of the Holy Ghost which is in you?

—**1 Corinthians 6:19**

89. Therefore glorify God in your body.
 —1 Corinthians 6:20

What a wonderful gift God gave you when He made your body! You use it to smell roses, to feel a kitten's fur, to taste chocolate, to hug someone's neck, to help a little child. Your body is so valuable to God, He calls it His holy place. He promises to help you use your body to do great things for Him.

90. We, being many, are one body in Christ, and everyone members one of another.
 —Romans 12:5

91. For, by one Spirit are we all baptized into one body.
 —1 Corinthians 12:13

When you are shy, you spend lots of time alone. But when you love and believe in Jesus, you don't need to feel lonely anymore. You have become a member of a great club, the body of believers. All the club members love Jesus, so they will love you, too. Being part of the body of Christ means loving and serving one another for Jesus' sake.

92. God will not suffer you to be tempted above that ye are able.
—1 Corinthians 10:13

93. But every man is tempted.
—James 1:14

Do you sometimes do wrong things, even when you do not want to? The Bible says that all of us have that problem. But there is a reason to be glad even when you struggle against temptation. God knows you, and

He will not allow more temptation that you can handle.

94. Lo, I am with you always, even unto the end of the world.
—**St. Matthew 28:20**

95. I am. . .the beginning and the end.
—**Revelation 21:6**

Many people worry about atomic bombs. They are now so powerful, they could blow up the entire world. But Jesus promises that we do not have to worry about this happening. He was here from the very beginning of the earth, and He will be with us, until the very end.

96. God hath given us a nail in his holy place.

—**Ezra 9:8**

97. If ye have faith as a grain of mustard seed,. . .nothing shall be impossible unto you.

—**St. Matthew 17:20**

"God can't love me. I don't have much faith," some people say. All it takes is a little. Faith only as big as one nail in the temple, or the size of a tiny seed, is all God needs from us. He promises to do great things if we will just believe in Him.

98. Yet will I leave a remnant.

—**Ezekiel 6:8**

99. Even so then at this present time also there is a remnant.

—**Romans 11:5**

100. The Lord shall. . .recover the remnant of his people.

—Isaiah 11:11

101. And I will gather the remnant of my flock.

—Jeremiah 23:3

A remnant is a leftover. God says He will always leave us leftovers. What does this curious promise mean?

Right now, in some parts of the world, people are being killed because they love God. Children are losing their parents. Parents weep as sons and daughters are taken from

them. If the punishment does not stop, all of God's people in those places could be wiped out. Will there be any left to love and worship Him? God promises He will tenderly gather the leftovers together and make them strong in Him. To people who are being persecuted, this promise brings great hope.

102. If they shall confess. . .their trespass,. . .then will I remember my covenant.

—**Leviticus 26:40,42**

103. If we confess our sins, he is faithful and just to forgive us our sins, and to cleanse us from all unrighteousness.

—**1 John 1:9**

The things we do to hurt others can make us feel terrible. Even after everyone else has forgotten, we kick ourselves over and over because of our sin. But God promises that He wants to forgive us. Tell Him you are truly sorry, and He will take away the terrible feeling of guilt.

104. Then opened he their understanding, that they might understand the Scripture.

—**St. Luke 24:45**

105. Thy words. . .giveth understanding unto the simple.

—**Psalm 119:130**

Does the Bible seem to you like a book written for aliens? Is it impossible to understand? Even Jesus' disciples needed help understanding the Scripture. But you can do what they did. Go to Jesus. Ask Him to help you as you read the Bible, and soon, the words won't seem so strange.

106. Not by might, nor by power, but by my spirit, saith the Lord of hosts.

—Zechariah 4:6

107. The Spirit. . .helpeth our weaknesses.

—Romans 8:26

What force does God use to do His work in the world? Could He send a wrestler to pin someone down? Could He equip an army with supernatural weapons? He has done both of those before. Most of the time, however, God uses something else: His Spirit and us. When we turn ourselves over to God, He turns our weakness into great power through His Spirit.

108. Therefore shall a man leave his father and his mother, and shall cleave

unto his wife: and they shall be one flesh.

—Genesis 2:24

109. They are no more twain, but one flesh.

—St. Matthew 19:6

**"They got married and lived happily ever after."
Many families don't have this kind of fairy-tale
life. Husbands and wives argue and fight. They
divorce. But God promises there is a better
way. His plan is to bring a husband and a wife
together in love so close, that they seem like
one body forever. Pray now that God will give
you this blessing when you grow up.**

110. He hath chosen us in him before the foundation of the world.

—Ephesians 1:4

111. God hath from the beginning chosen you to salvation.

—2 Thessalonians 2:13

112. Come,. . . inherit the kingdom prepared for you from the foundation of the world.

—St. Matthew 25:34

113. I have chosen you out of the world.

—**St. John 15:19**

Have you ever been the last one to be picked for a playground game? It's so embarrassing! But there is Someone who chose you first, even before the world was made. Why did God pick you for His team? It isn't because you are such a good person. All human beings are sinners. God picked you just because He wanted to. It is good to know that, long before you ever thought about God, He was thinking about you and choosing you.

Some people don't want to be chosen. They don't want to be on God's team. This makes God very sad, for He knows they will miss all the blessings He has prepared for His own.

114. God is love.

—1 John 4:16

115. He that dwelleth in love dwelleth in God.

—1 John 4:16

One of the best things in life is a good dog. He waits by the door for you to come home from school. When he sees you, he barks and jumps up and down and licks your face. At night in bed, he snugggles at your feet and keeps you warm. When a dog loves you, he loves you all over. God's love is the same way. When you know even a little of His love, you feel it all over!

116. By this shall all men know that ye are my disciples, if ye have love one to another.

—St. John 13:35

117. But the fruit of the Spirit is love.
—**Galatians 5:22**

When God tells us to love one another, He does not expect us to do it on our own. By ourselves, it is very hard to love someone we do not even like. But when we give our hearts to God, His Spirit comes to live in us and helps us love others— even the boy down the street who teases and throws stones!

118. For the eyes of the Lord run to and fro throughout the whole world.
—**2 Chronicles 16:9**

119. The eyes of the Lord are in every place, beholding the evil and the good.
—**Proverbs 15:3**

120. The ways of man are before the eyes of the Lord.

—Proverbs 5:21

121. Thy Father. . .seeth in secret.

—St. Matthew 6:18

Every time the class bully picks on you, the teacher is out of the room. No one sees when you get kicked under the cafeteria table. Where are your parents when your sister breaks a dish and blames it on you?

Even the most watchful person misses important things. Evil deeds are done every day, and no one sees. No one sees, that is, but God. He promises that nothing happens on earth that He does not see. He sees things that are done out in the open, and He see things that are done behind closed doors. We do not have to worry that evil deeds will go unpunished because no one saw them happen. God sees, and He will deal with them.

122. And Noah built an altar unto the Lord;. . .And the Lord smelled a sweet savor.

—**Genesis 8:20,21**

123. For we are unto God a sweet savor.

—**2 Corinthians 2:15**

M-m-m-m! Good smells make us happy. When Noah made an offering of thanksgiving, it smelled good to God. The Lord promises that when we live lives of obedience and love, we will smell sweet to Him. Make it your goal to be a pleasant fragrance to God every day!

124. Except when the Lord builds the house, the laborers build in vain.
—**Psalm 127:1**

125. Whosoever heareth these sayings of mine, and doeth them, I will liken him unto a wise man, which built his house upon a rock.
—**St. Matthew 7:24**

126 . He that built all things is God.
—**Hebrews 3:4**

Building a strong house is hard work. Building a strong life is, too. Make sure God is the architect of your life. Then your house is sure to stand, no matter what storms may come.

127. The tongue is a fire,. . .and setteth on fire the course of nature.

—James 3:6

128. But the tongue can no man tame.

—James 3:8

129. I have put my words in thy mouth.

—Isaiah 51:16

130. Let the words of
my mouth. . .be
acceptable in thy
sight, O Lord.

—Psalm 19:14

Even though the tongue is a very small body part, it can do enormous damage.

How many friendships have crashed and burned because of your tongue? The Bible says there is only One who can tame the tongue. The next time you are angry and cruel words rush into your mouth, stop. Think. Pray. When you offer your mouth to God, He promises to fill it with words of truth and blessing and love.

131. Take my yoke upon you, and learn of me.

—St. Matthew 11:29

132. For my yoke is easy and my burden is light.

—St. Matthew 11:30

A yoke is the wooden harness that goes over a horse so it can pull a plow. When we love Jesus, we are to wear His harness. But

He promises that the work He has for us to do will be joyful, not burdensome.

133. Whatsoever a man soweth, that shall he also reap.

—Galatians 6:7

134. To him that soweth righteousness shall be a sure reward.

—Proverbs 11:18

Sowing and reaping are farm words. Sowing means planting, and reaping is harvesting. God promises that the deeds we plant in life will grow up to give us their harvest. Good deeds will produce a goodly harvest. Evil deeds will only grow more evil. Today, we might express the same idea this way: "You get what you pay for."

135. But many that are first shall be last, and the last shall be first.

—St. Matthew 19:30

136. If any man desire to be first, the same shall be last of all, and servant of all.

—St. Mark 9:35

137. Thus saith the Lord; I am the first, and I am the last; and beside me there is no God.

—Isaiah 44:6

138. I am the first and the last.

—Revelation 1:17

Are you the baby in your family? It doesn't seem fair— the youngest child is always the last to do everything! The disciples complained about this, too. None of them wanted to be last. Each wanted to be the greatest,  the most important among all of Jesus' followers. But Jesus' words and his actions taught the disciples a new way of thinking.

First, He told them that they had things

backwards. In God's Kingdom, He said, it is more important to be last, to put everyone else first. Then He showed them how. Jesus Himself, the first, most important being in all the universe, was willing to be last among men, to serve others, even to die on the cross. Jesus promises that those who are last on earth will be first in Heaven.

139. It is better to hear the rebuke of the wise, than for a man to hear the song of fools.

—Ecclesiastes 7:5

140. Fear ye not the reproach of men, neither be ye afraid of their revilings.

—Isaiah 51:7

Do you have trouble taking criticism? Many of us do. But God promises that we will grow and improve if we listen to advice. Wise advice, that is. Criticism that is cruel or tears us down is not wise advice. God says that He will never let harmful words stop His people.

141. Be ye doers of the Word.
—James 1:22

142. Even a child is known by his doings.
—Proverbs 20:11

"I'm just a kid. It doesn't matter what I do or say." This is not what God thinks! He cares very much about everything you do or say. In fact, He promises that even now, as a child, you have all that you need to do great things, things that will matter forever. You have His Word, and you can start living by it. So, what are you waiting for? Be a Doer!

143. Thou shalt love the Lord thy God . . .with all thy mind.
—St. Luke 10:27

144. Serve him. . .with a willing mind.
—**1 Chronicles 28:9**

145. Be ye transformed by the renewing of your mind.
—**Romans 12:2**

146. Thou wilt keep him in perfect peace, whose mind is stayed on thee.
—**Isaiah 26:3**

"Do I think much about God? No, I have more important things on my mind."

Some people believe thinking has nothing to do with faith in God. But anyone who has read the Bible or prayed knows differently. God promises He will change us into new, better people when we put our minds on Him. We can take our hardest questions to God. He will stretch our thinking with incredible new ideas. And along the way, God says, He will give us peace of mind. That is something even many smart people never find on their own.

147. A good name is rather to be chosen than great riches.

—**Proverbs 22:1**

148. A good name is better than precious ointment.

—**Ecclesiastes 7:1**

Your reputation is invisible, but it is very valuable. It cannot be bought or sold. You earn it by your actions and attitudes. Once you have a reputation, good or bad, it is not easily changed. That is why the Bible says to take care of your reputation. Make sure people think of good things when they hear your name. You will never be sorry, God promises!

149. For now we see through a glass, darkly, but then face to face. Now I know in part; but then shall I know even as also I am known.

—1 Corinthians 13:12

150. O the depth of the riches both of the wisdom and knowledge of God!

—Romans 11:33

Have you ever tried to read, wearing glasses that were smudged? You can only see a little of the print on the page! That's how it is with our understanding of God. Now, in our life on earth, we know only a small bit. Some day, when we are in Heaven with Him, we will understand everything. And that knowledge will make us feel very, very rich!

151. Lay not up for yourselves treasures upon earth, where moth and rust doth corrupt, and where thieves break through and steal.

—St. Matthew 6:19

152. But lay up for yourselves treasures in heaven, where neither moth nor rust doth corrupt, and where thieves do not break through nor steal.

—St. Matthew 6:20

153. For where your treasure is, there will your heart be also.

—St. Matthew 6:21

Moths eat fancy sweaters. Bicycles rust. Money can be stolen. But Jesus promises that the riches we deposit in the Bank of Heaven will be safe forever. What are these riches? A true story from history gives us the answer.

Long ago, enemy soldiers broke into a church where believers were gathered. Waving their swords, the soldiers demanded to see the church's treasure. They could not wait to fill their pockets with gold and jewels. But instead, one of the believers pointed to the orphan children, the sick and the elderly sitting among them.

"These," the believer said, "are our treasures."

The loving deeds we do for others are riches that will never rust.

154. I was hungry, and ye gave me meat: I was thirsty, and ye gave me drink: I was a stranger, and ye took me in.

—St. Matthew 25:35

155. Inasmuch as ye have done it unto the least of these my brethren, ye have done it unto me.

—**St. Matthew 25:40**

If you want to make a father happy, do something nice for his child. It is the same way with our Heavenly Father. When we help one of his children who is in need, He rejoices. Being kind to others here on earth is the way we can send a gift of love to God.

156. Knock, and the door shall be opened.

—St. Luke 11:9

157. Behold, I stand at the door and knock. **—Revelation 3:20**

Imagine that there is a door between Heaven and earth. When we want to know Jesus, all we have to do is knock on that door. He promises that He will immediately come to meet us. There are other times when we are not looking for Jesus, but He stands waiting on the other side. He knocks and knocks and does not stop until we open the door and invite Him into our lives.

158. A friend loveth at all times.

—Proverbs 17:17

159. A man that hath friends must show himself friendly.

—Proverbs 18:24

160. Iron sharpeneth iron; so a man sharpeneth the countenance of his friend.

—Proverbs 27:17

161. A threefold cord is not quickly broken.

—Ecclesiastes 4:12

God makes some very basic promises about friendship. If you are kind and friendly, He says, you will make many friends. But then God goes further. He explains how having the right friends can make you a better person.

You know you have a good friend when being with that person sharpens you— makes you smarter or stronger in a healthy way. Spending time with the wrong friend, on the other hand, would be like cutting with a dull knife. It could hurt your school-work, or give you a bad attitude. God also says that good friends can help you stand firm in your beliefs. Make two friends who want to love and serve God. Together, you can be an unbreakable cord of three!

162. The beauty of old men is the gray head.

—Proverbs 20:29

163. The gray head is a crown of glory, if it be found in the way of right-eousness.

—Proverbs 16:31

These two promises may not mean much to you right now, but someday they will. It is never too early to think about the kind of old person you want to be. Decide now to live a life of obedience to God.

Then He will give you a reward as precious to Him as a crown— gray hair!

164. Thou shalt. . .be a crown of glory in the hand of the Lord.

—**Isaiah 62:3**

165. Henceforth there is laid up for me a crown of righteousness.

—**2 Timothy 4:8**

Have you ever dreamed of being a king, of wearing a crown covered with jewels? Most of us will never wear crowns here on earth, but God promises things will be different in heaven. There is a crown waiting for each person who loves and believes in God, a crown not of jewels, but gleaming with good deeds and faithfulness.

166. Boast not thyself of tomorrow; for thou knowest not what a day may bring forth.

—**Proverbs 27:1**

167. But let him that boasteth in this, that he understandeth and knoweth me.

—Jeremiah 9:24

168. But God forbid that I should boast, save in the cross of our Lord Jesus Christ.

—Galatians 6:14

169. My soul shall make her boast in the Lord.

—**Psalm 34:2**

No one likes to listen to a braggart. "I'm the greatest!" he boasts. "I have all the best things, and I can do better than you." The Bible reminds the boaster that things can change overnight. The person crowing at the top of the heap today may find himself at the very bottom tomorrow. There is only one time when it is all right to boast— when you are talking about the Lord Jesus. Share the good news with someone today. "Jesus is the greatest! He has forgiven my sins, and I will live with Him forever!"

170. If. . .God so clothe the grass, . . . how much more will he clothe you?

—**St. Luke 12:28**

171. But put. . .on the Lord Jesus Christ.

—**Romans 13:14**

Even in biblical times, people worried about clothes and how to pay for them. Jesus came to create a new style. He wanted to see people who were beautiful, not because of the clothes they wore on their bodies, but because of the love they wore in their hearts. Tomorrow, when you get up and reach into your closet, put on Jesus. You will be truly well-dressed.

172. Zacchaeus, make haste, and come down; for today I must abide at thy house.

—St. Luke 19:5

173. I will come into him, and will sup with him, and he with me.

—Revelation 3:20

One way families celebrate their love for each other is by eating meals together. We relax, and laugh, and talk, and stay at the table long after supper is over. Zacchaeus, the dishonest little tax collector, was amazed that Jesus wanted to spend time with him this way. That supper changed his life forever.

Jesus promises He wants to have the same special time with each one of us. Invite Him into your life today!

174. Thou openest thine hand and satisfiest the desire of every living thing.

—Psalm 145:16

175. Delight thyself. . .in the Lord; and he shall give thee the desires of thine heart.

—Psalm 37:4

176. The desire of the righteous shall be granted.

Proverbs 10:24

177. Desire spiritual gifts.

—Corinthians 14:1

Our Heavenly Father wants His children to be happy, to have all the best things. The problem is, our idea of best is often very different from His. We desire material things: a new stereo, a faster car, more toys, nicer clothes. But God promises that when we learn to enjoy Him, our desires will be for those things that truly are the best: love, joy, peace, patience, kindness, goodness, faithfulness, gentleness, and self-control.

Is there something you lack, something you

desire deep in your heart? Talk to God about it. Listen for His answer. Be patient, and know that whatever happens, it is God's very best for you.

178. Every good tree bringeth forth good fruit.

—St. Matthew 7:17

179. I have chosen you. . .that ye should go and bring forth fruit.

—St. John 15:16

180. I am the vine, ye are the branches.

—St. John 15:5

Being a young man or woman of God means producing good fruit for Him. Growing Godly fruit can be hard. We think of good deeds to do, but never quite get around to doing them. We decide to help someone, and it backfires. Our fruit for God ends up sour and rotten. What is wrong?

If we are not producing good fruit, it means we are not drawing our nourishment from Jesus, the Vine. Let Him tell you when to help someone. Listen when He whispers about your attitude. Stay close to Jesus, and He will grow wonderful fruit in you!

181. Ponder the path of thy feet, and let all thy ways be established.

—Proverbs 4:26

182. How beautiful are the feet of them that preach the gospel of peace.

—Romans 10:15

Only God could love feet! He blesses feet that walk carefully down safe, healthy paths. When feet are the very dirtiest, from taking news of Him to others, He calls them beautiful. So forget about expensive shoes and fancy socks. Just have missionary feet!

183. I have covered thee in the shadow of mine hand.

—Isaiah 51:16

184. In the shadow of thy wings I will rejoice.

—Psalm 63:7

On a scorching summer day, the shadow of a big tree is a good place to rest. When you are scared or sad, God's shadow is a good place to rest. Close your eyes and think of a big strong hand gently sheltering you from trouble. Rest there in the cool safety. That's how God's love and protection feels.

185. For whosoever shall call upon the name of the Lord shall be saved.
— **Romans 10:13**

186. For there is none other name under heaven given among men, whereby we must be saved.
— **Acts 4:12**

There is saving power in the name of Jesus. When you call out to Him, He will hear you and give you life with Him forever. Many people think other gods can do this as well. But the Bible promises that this kind of power is given to just one, the True Holy One, the Lord Jesus Christ.

187. The Holy Ghost. . .shall bring all things to your remembrance.
—**St. John 14:26**

188. My mouth shall praise thee with joyful lips: when I remember thee upon my bed.
—**Psalm 63:6**

What do you think about, in bed at night before you go to sleep? This time is special to God. He uses it to help you remember, to think back over your day. Did your words and deeds honor Him? Let your last thoughts each day be praise and thanksgiving to Him.

189. All the tribes of the earth. . shall see the Son. . .coming in the clouds of heaven with power and great glory.

—**St. Matthew 24:30**

190. And his feet shall stand in that day upon the Mount of Olives, which is before Jerusalem.

—**Zechariah 14:4**

Give Thanks

191. Be ye therefore ready also; for the Son. . .cometh at an hour when ye think not.

—**St. Luke 12:40**

The Bible gives us very specific promises about the future. God wants us to know what will happen, so that we will not be afraid.

First, God promises that Jesus will return to the earth, and that everyone will see Him coming down from Heaven. What a tremendous sight that will be! He will go back to the place on earth where He walked and talked with His first followers, the land of Israel. We do not know, however, when this will happen. God tells us to always be ready, for Jesus will come when we least expect Him. We should live in readiness, to greet Him any day.

192. Blessed are they that do his commandments, that they may have right to the tree of life; and may enter in through the gates into the city.

—Revelation 22:14

193. They are before the throne of God, and serve him day and night in his temple; and he that sitteth on the throne shall dwell among them.

—**Revelation 7:15**

Have you ever wondered what Heaven will be like? God tells us something about it, in the last book of the Bible, Revelation. He describes Heaven as a great city, with gates and a temple. The tree of life grows there, and in the very center of the heavenly city stands His throne. All who love and believe in Him will come into the city, to worship, to serve and to live with the Lord forever.

Would you like to know more? Revelation is filled with fascinating details. Read from it today!

194. They that turn many to righteous
-ness shall shine as the stars forever
and ever.

—Daniel 12:3

195. Then shall the righteous shine
forth as the sun.

—St. Matthew 13:43

**Today, many young people dream of being
stars— movie stars, or famous athletes. But
God promises something even better, for
those who live holy lives, helping others.
They will shine with a brightness that will
never fade. How many athletes and movie
stars can say that?**

196. God loveth a cheerful giver.

—2 Corinthians 9:7

197. Give, and it shall be given unto
you; good measure, pressed down,
and shaken together, and running
over.

It is disappointing to buy ice cream where they serve skimpy scoops. We look for the place where they dip deep and pack the ice cream way down in the cone. That's what God looks for, too. He promises that when we give generously to those in need, He will give generously to us.

198. Whatsoever things are true, whatsoever things are honest, whatsoever things are just, whatsoever things are of good report; if there be any virtue, and if there be any praise, think on these things,. . .and the God of peace shall be with you.

—Philippians 4:8-9

GIGO is computer slang. It stands for, "Garbage in, garbage out." In other words, a computer is only as good as the information it is fed. God promises that our minds work the same way. Do we want to live good lives?

Then we must fill our minds with the things that are true and good and right.

Today, it is easy to feed our brains a steady diet of mindless cartoons, violent movies, negative music and ugly language. It is all around us, on almost every channel. But with determination and real effort, we can turn it off. Pull the plug. Read a good book. Go home when friends want to rent an R-rated movie. Spend time with your family instead. You are the only one who can police your mind. Keep it clean, so God will be happy to live there.

199. A man that beareth false witness against his neighbor is a maul, and a sword, and a sharp arrow.

—Proverbs 25:1

200. The lip of truth shall be established forever; but a lying tongue is but for a moment.

—**Proverbs 12:19**

Have you ever been hurt by a lie? Then you know lies can do as much damage as any weapon. They can destroy friendships and families, and ruin good reputations. But God tells us that lies cannot last. Sooner or later, the truth always comes out. He promises to see that it does.

201. Remember now thy Creator in the days of thy youth.

—**Ecclesiastes 12:1**

202. Those that seek me early shall find me.

—**Proverbs 8:17**

"Go to church? Oh, there will be plenty of time for that later, when I am older. Right now, I am too busy having fun to make room for God in my life."

God gives each of us the opportunity to meet Him. If we put Him off, we cannot be certain we will have another chance. Accidents happen. Things change. Hearts grow angry and hard. Don't put off your meeting with the Lord. Get to know Him now, and grow up with Him by your side.

203. Ye were sealed with that holy Spirit of promise.

—**Ephesians 1:13**

204. Ye are sealed unto the day of redemption.

—**Ephesians 4:30**

The label on an aspirin bottle reads, "Sealed for your protection." God does the same thing for us. Once we love and believe in Him, he seals us off, so sin cannot infect our hearts. That seal, the Holy Spirit, is His guarantee. No matter how much sin surrounds us, the seal will not give way until the end of time, when God brings us to live with Him forever.

205. With God nothing shall be impossible.

—**St. Luke 1:37**

206. All things are possible to him that believeth.

—**St. Mark 9:23**

Nothing is too difficult for the Lord! When we believe in Him, His power and His plans flow through us. Be open-minded about what He wants to do with you, even when it seems impossible. That word is simply not in God's vocabulary!

207. And we know that all things work together for good to them that love God.

—Romans 8:28

208. We glory in tribulation, . . .knowing that tribulation worketh patience; and patience, experience; and experience, hope.

—Romans 5:3-4

For unbelievers, trouble is— just trouble. But for those who trust in God, trouble can be the place where good things start. God tells us to be glad when we face problems, because they teach us to be patient and calm. Patience produces strength of character. Because we are strong, we trust God even more than we did in the beginning. Only in God's math can troubles add up to great blessing.

209. The wages of sin is death.
—Romans 6:23

210. But the gift of God is eternal life through Jesus Christ our Lord.
—Romans 6:23

Those who look to the Lord and His Son Jesus Christ receive an incredible bonus that begins now and continues forever— eternal life.

211. These six things doth the Lord hate: yea, seven are an abomination unto him.
—Proverbs 6:16

212. A proud look, a lying tongue, and hands that shed innocent blood.

—Proverbs 6:17

213. An heart that deviseth wicked imaginations, feet that be swift in running to mischief.

—Proverbs 6:18

214. A false witness that speaketh lies, and he that soweth discord among brethren.

—Proverbs 6:19

A picky teacher can be hard to please. We make many mistakes until we learn exactly what she wants. But God is different. He spells out the seven behaviors that He hates the most. We can be sure that He will never change His mind about them. Do you know what NOT to do?

God hates:

1) a bad attitude
2) lying
3) murdering
4) planning evil deeds
5) being eager to do wrong
6) giving false information on purpose
7) stirring up trouble in the family

215. I came not to call the righteous, but sinners to repentance.

—St. Mark 2:17

216. For the Son. . .came to seek and to save that which was lost.

—St. Luke 19:10

217. While we were yet sinners, Christ died for us.

—Romans 5:8

"I'm not good enough for Jesus. Let me clean up my life, get my act together first. Then I will work on getting to know Him."

Some people want to treat Jesus as if He were only fancy company. They want to put a white cloth and silver on the table before they ask Him into their lives. But Jesus does not want to wait. We do not have to be perfect before we invite Him in. He is ready to come and help right now, while the supper is burning and the milk is sour and the house is a mess and the family is fighting, again!

218. In returning and rest shall ye be saved.

—Isaiah 30:15

219. Return unto me, and I will return unto you, saith the Lord of hosts.

—**Malachi 3:7**

220. Return, ye backsliding children, and I will heal your backslidings.

—**Jeremiah 3:22**

221. Return unto me; for I have redeemed thee.

—**Isaiah 44:22**

Backsliding sounds like some kind of playground game. But it is nothing to fool around with. Backsliding is what pulls us away from God. It is all of the old bad habits that keep trying to regain control of our lives. These old habits are very strong, and they call out to us long after we have quit them. Many times, we do not even realize we are sliding. We wake up one morning deep in old sin— again.

What if this happens to you? Can you ever go back to God? He says, "Yes!" He will wait patiently until you come to your senses. The minute you turn back to Him, He will give you rest and healing.

222. I am come that they might have life, and that they might have it more abundantly.

—St. John 10:10

223. Out of the abundance of the heart, the mouth speaketh.

—St. Matthew 12:34

A car with high-test gas in its tank is a happy car. It runs at peak performance. Its engine purrs. That's how we act when Jesus fills us with His abundance. We find new joy and fulfillment in our ordinary days. Our hearts overflow with thanksgiving, and we can't wait to tell others the reason why.

224. Abide in me, and I in you.

—St. John 15:4

225. And now, little children, abide in him;. . that. . .we may have confidence.

—1 John 2:28

One of the first words you teach a dog is, "Stay!" Learning this word keeps the dog focused. He watches you, his master, no matter what else is going on. The animal develops self-control and confidence. Jesus promises this to us if we will learn to abide, to stay always in him.

226. Hath the Lord as great delight in burnt offerings and sacrifices, as in obeying the voice of the Lord? Behold, to obey is better than sacrifice.

—1 Samuel 15:22

227. Present your bodies a living sacrifice, holy, acceptable unto God, which is your reasonable service.

—Romans 12:1

228. The sacrifices of God are a broken spirit: a broken and a contrite heart.

—Psalm 51:17

229. To do good and to communicate forget not: for with such sacrifices God is well-pleased.

—**Hebrews 12:16**

What would you like to give to God— a million dollars, a beautiful stained glass window, an airplane for missionaries to use? Someday God may lead you to give Him all of those things. But there is something else He longs for, something you can give Him right now: yourself. This is the gift that God treasures the very most.

First, give Him a heart broken over your sin. Give him a body that tries to obey His commands and teachings each day. Give him a mouth that communicates kind words to others. These are the offerings that delight the Lord.

230. By one man sin entered into the world, and death by sin.

—**Romans 5:12**

231. There is therefore now no condemnation to them which are in Christ Jesus.

—**Romans 8:1**

Sin is like a deadly disease. Once Adam sinned, the disease entered his body, to be passed down to all his descendants. That's why every human being sins. It's in our nature. But because Jesus took the punishment for our sin, God declares us, "Not guilty!"

232. He is a rewarder of them that diligently seek him.

—**Hebrews 11:6**

233. Study to show thyself approved unto God, a workman that needeth not to be ashamed, rightly dividing the word of truth.

—2 Timothy 2:15

It is easy to become part of the family of God. Just believe, and love Him. It is hard work, however, to know all about God. We must study His Word carefully and sincerely to learn all we can. Open your Bible today. Ask the Lord to help you get to know Him better. He promises to grant your request.

234. Be not forgetful to entertain strangers; for thereby some have entertained angels unawares.

—Hebrews 13:2

235. Use hospitality one to another without grudging.

—1 Peter 4:9

Wouldn't it be fun to have dinner with an angel? God says that could happen, for His angels are all around us. Often, they appear as ordinary human beings. So be kind and friendly to those in need. Share generously of what you have. Look for the touch of God in each person you meet. You just might find an angel!

236. In Christ are hid all the treasures of wisdom and knowledge.

—Colossians 2:3

237. Hold thy peace and I will teach thee wisdom.

—Job 33:33

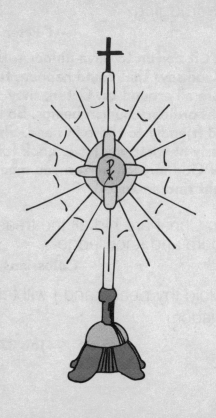

Teachers pile on the homework. Parents urge us to work harder. We take piano and dance and karate lessons. The pressure to be smart is huge. But often, we forget to start at the right place— with God. All knowledge is His, and when we quietly begin with Him, He will open our minds.

238. All Scripture is given by inspiration of God.

—2 Timothy 3:16

239. For the prophecy came not in old time by the will of man: but holy men of God spoke as they were moved by the Holy Ghost.

—2 Peter 1:21

240. What ye hear in the ear, that preach ye upon the housetops.

—St. Matthew 10:27

How can we be sure that the Bible is true? First of all, we have God's word on it. Through hundreds of years, using many different writers, God gave the same message over and over again. What is true in the book of Genesis is true in the book of Revelation. History also proves the truth of the Bible. Dates and events mentioned in Scripture have been confirmed by other ancient records and by archeological finds.

But the most important proof of all is in your own heart. Read the Bible sincerely. Look for what it has to say about your own life. Then ask God to show you if these things are true. Just as He spoke to the men who wrote down the words of the Bible, He will speak to you.

You will know, beyond any doubt, that God's Word is truth.

241. As arrows are in the hand of a mighty man; so are the children of thy youth.

—Psalm 127:4

242. But Samuel ministered before the Lord, being a child.

—1 Samuel 2:18

Many adults pay little attention to the things children can do. But in God's hand, even a child can be a powerful weapon for good. Young Samuel served the Lord more faithfully than did the older priests around him. God used the boy to begin a clean-up campaign that called people back to true and right ways. What does God want to do with you?

243. For our God is a consuming fire.
—**Hebrews 12:29**

244. Behold, I will make my words in thy mouth fire.

—**Jeremiah 5:14**

Before you use a needle to remove a splinter, you sterilize it with fire. God promises to burn away the sin in our lives. He will also use our mouths to speak His cleansing words to others. God's fire has enormous power. Handle it with great respect and care.

245. Every pot in Jerusalem and in Judah shall be holiness unto the Lord of hosts.

—**Zechariah 14:20**

246. Behold, as the clay is in the potter's hand, so are ye in mine hand.

—**Jeremiah 18:6**

247. Hath not the potter power over the clay?

—**Romans 9:21**

248. For dust thou art, and unto dust shalt thou return.

—**Genesis 3:19**

Clay is made of the dust of the earth. God reminds us that we are His clay. It is good to know that His skilled hand is at work, shaping us into better people. Some He forms as beautiful china. These people are like the dishes used for parties and important

dinners. Others of us He shapes into everyday pots. We hold flowers and food and leftovers. But no matter how God shapes us, He calls us holy. We are special to Him, and set apart for His purpose. The next time you feel dull and ordinary, just remember: You are pottery of great promise!

249. In the midst of the throne stood a Lamb.

—Revelation 5:6

250. Four and twenty elders fell down before the Lamb, having every one golden vials full of odors, which are the prayers of saints.

—Revelation 5:8

251. And he showed me a pure river of water of life, clear as crystal, proceeding out of the throne of God.

—Revelation 22:1

252. The twelve gates were twelve pearls:. . .and the street of the city was pure gold, as it were transparent glass.
—**Revelation 21:21**

When the disciple John was an old man, God gave him a very special gift. It was a vision of Heaven. The things John saw were almost too great for words, but God told him to write the vision down. That way, everyone could read and know what Heaven will be like.

Some things John saw are puzzling. Why does Heaven need so many gates? What does transparent gold look like? Other things are exciting. God saves all of our prayers up in Heaven, in golden bowls of incense. The river of living water that flows into every believer's heart starts at the very throne of God. And best of all, we will see Jesus. He will be on the throne, the nail marks from the cross showing on his hands and feet. How wonderful a promise, to bow before Him in love and worship!

253. Come ye after me, and I will make you to become fishers of men.
—St. Mark 1:17

254. The kingdom of heaven is like unto a net.

—St. Matthew 13:47

Catching fish is great fun. Jesus promises that believers will get to go fishing with Him. He wants to gather everyone into His net, to live with Him forever. Our job is to throw out a line, to share what we know, to pull up someone who is struggling. Good fishermen are always prepared, and they stay on the alert. Are you ready? Let's go fish— with Jesus!

255. Every perfect gift is from above, and cometh down from the Father of lights.

—James 1:17

256. As every man hath received the gift, even so minister the same one to another.

—1 Peter 4:10

We all love to get presents. God promises us perfect gifts. He gives them for two reasons. First, His gifts prove His love. Then, His gifts help us to help others. Has God given you a passion for sports? Enjoy that gift, and use it to share godly sportsmanship with your friends. God's gifts never quit giving!

257. His banner over me was love.

—**Song of Solomon 2:4**

258. Thou hast given a banner to them that fear thee, that it may be displayed because of the truth.

—**Psalm 60:4**

259. He will lift up a banner to the nations from far.

—**Isaiah 5:26**

260. And the Lord shall save. . .his people: for they shall be. . .lifted up as a banner upon his land.

—**Zechariah 9:16**

A colorful flag flying high in the sky is hard to miss. Everyone's eye is drawn to it. In battle, soldiers press on, following their flag. Explorers look for new lands where they can plant their country's flag.

God says His love is a huge flag over us. We can fly it proudly, because it stands for the truth. When we live as God's people, we ourselves are like flags. Everywhere we go, others look at us because we stand for God.

So square your shoulders. Stand straight and tall. Live according to God's Word. Be his banner to the world.

261. Consider the work of God: for who can make that straight, which he hath made crooked?

—**Ecclesiastes 6:13**

262. The crooked shall be made straight, and the rough places plain.

—**Isaiah 40:4**

Hair that is naturally curly always curls. You can cut it off, or straighten it, but it will always grow back curly. Did you choose to  have curly hair? No, God chose it for you. What if you don't like having curly hair? Then you are rejecting something that God Himself planned just for you. We don't always understand His choices: freckles, crooked teeth, our skin, a physical problem.

But we know that some day in Heaven, all will be made right.

263. And it shall come to pass,... that I will pour out my spirit upon all flesh, and your sons and your daughters shall prophesy, your old men shall dream dreams, your young men shall see visions.

—Joel 2:28

Some people worry because God does not speak to them in dreams and visions, the way He did to people long ago. But we have God's written word, the Bible, and we have God's Spirit in our hearts, to speak to us. God will continue speaking to His people until the very last day, when Jesus will make all things clear to us.

264. Wash me, and I shall be whiter than snow.
                                        —**Psalm 51:7**

265. Though your sins be as scarlet, they shall be as white as snow.
                                        —**Isaiah 1:18**

266. Lift up your eyes, and look on the fields; for they are white already to harvest.
                                        —**St. John 4:35**

267. He that overcometh. . .shall be clothed in white robes.
                                        —**Revelation 3:5**

In Bible times, white things were special. Good soap was hard to get, so nothing stayed clean for long. That's why these promises meant so much to believers. They still tell us

what God does for those who love Him.

Sin makes us dirty. It covers us with a deep, dark stain. But when we go to God for forgiveness, He takes away the stain. It feels so good to be clean, we want to go and tell others how they can be washed. Jesus promises that when we do, the fields will be as if they were full of white flowers ready to pick. Many will listen and believe. Then in Heaven, we will be given beautiful white robes. Long ago, only the wealthiest people could afford white. They would wear garments only a day or two, until they got dirty. Then they would buy new ones. When we understand God's "white" promises, we see how meaningful they are.

268. The wolf. . .shall dwell with the lamb, and the leopard shall lie down with the kid.

—Isaiah 11:6

269. The desert shall rejoice, and blossom as the rose.

—**Isaiah 35:1**

270. The parched ground shall become a pool.

—**Isaiah 35:7**

The book of Genesis tells us that in the beginning, all the animals got along with each other. God provided plants for them to eat, and they came peaceably to Adam to receive their names. But then sin entered the world. Creature turned against creature. The wolf became the enemy of the lamb. The leopard saw the kid as a tasty meal.

But God promises that one day in the future, all things will return to their original state. The animals will live together in peace as God intended in the beginning. Dry places will spring to life with lush growth. Wastelands will become fertile fields. Nothing— not man, not the animals, not the plants, not even the hills or the mountains— will suffer any more from the infection of sin.

271. It is easier for a camel to go through the eye of a needle, than for a rich man to enter into the kingdom of God.

—St. Mark 10:25

272. Neither their silver nor their gold shall be able to deliver them in the day of the Lord's wrath.

—Zephaniah 1:18

It's impossible for a camel to go through a needle's eye. Does that mean there is no room in Heaven for wealthy people? No. **Silver and gold can buy nice things here on earth, but they are worthless in God's kingdom. Make sure you pay as much attention to your faith account as you do to your bank account.**

273. A new heart also will I give you, and a new spirit will I put within you: and I will take away the stony heart out of your flesh, and I will give you a heart of flesh.

—Ezekiel 36:27

When a shoe does not fit properly, it can make a hard spot form on your foot. The same thing can happen with your heart. Problems make it grow hard. You have no tenderness there for God or anyone else. But God promises you a heart transplant. He will make sure you stay soft and tenderhearted so you can love others.

274. That all the people pf the earth might know the hand of the Lord. . . is mighty.

—Joshua 4:24

275. Neither shall any man pluck them out of my Father's hand.

—St. John 10:28

276. Behold, my hands and feet.

—St. Luke 24:39

277. For day and night, thy hand was heavy upon me.

—Psalm 32:4

Think for a moment about God's hands. They are skillful. They have shaped the world so everyone can know of His creativity and His power. His hands are gentle and strong. They hold tightly those who love Him, protecting them from danger.

Jesus' hands are loving. They show the marks where His enemies nailed him to the cross. His death paid the price for our sins. The Holy Spirit's hands are ever-present. They touch us when we need to remember, when we need to think about our sins.

They wake us up so we can do God's will. They nudge us to speak kind words. When we give ourselves to the Lord, we're always in good hands!

In The Name Of Peace

278. The eternal God is thy refuge, and underneath are the everlasting arms.

—**Deuteronomy 33:27**

279. I have made, and I will bear; even I will carry, and will deliver you.

—**Isaiah 46:4**

When you are so tired and discouraged, that you cannot take another step, remember – God's arms are always there. He promises to hold you, to carry you and to make sure you reach a safe place. His arms will never get tired. You can depend on Him.

280. There shall be showers of blessing.

—Ezekiel 34:26

281. And all these blessings shall
come on thee, . . . if thou shalt hear-
ken unto the voice of the Lord thy God.

—Deuteronomy 28:2

**Look out the window the next time it rains.
Let the drops remind you of all God's blessings. For each drop, name a blessing— if
you can keep up. God showers us with so
much goodness, it is like a downpour. There
are simply too many blessings to count.
How good he is to His people!**

282. If any man thirst, let him come unto
me and drink.

—St. John 7:37

283. Whosoever drinketh from the water
that I shall give him shall never thirst.

—St. John 4:14

284. Therefore with joy shall ye draw water out of the wells of salvation.

—**Isaiah 12:3**

Our bodies are 65% water. Water is an important part of the chemical reactions that keep us alive; respiration, digestion, circulation. Drinking enough water is absolutely essential for our health.

Perhaps that is why God uses water as an important symbol in Scripture. Just as our bodies need water for physical life, our spirits thirst for the water that gives eternal life. Jesus invites us to drink Him in. When we do, He promises that we will be wonderfully satisfied. Our spirits will never be thirsty again.

285. For he shall give his angels charge river thee, to keep thee in all thy ways.

—**Psalm 91:11**

286. The Lord . . . will send his angel with thee, and prosper thy way. —**Genesis 24:40**

287. But the angel of the Lord by night opened the prison doors.

—**Acts 5:19**

288. The chariots of God are twenty thousand, even thousands of angels.

—**Psalm**

Gods angels are everywhere, thousands and thousand of angels! They watch over us and protect us. They help us in all we do. An angel freed the missionary Paul when he was in prison. Angels brought important messages to Abraham, to Mary and to the shepherds on the hills of Bethlehem. An angel fought for the people of Israel during Daniel's day, and an angel prepared Gideon's heart for battle.

The next time you feel scared or lonely or helpless, just remember. There is an angel watching out for you!

289. This is the day which the Lord hath made; we will rejoice and be glad in it.

—**Psalm 118:24**

290. The day of the Lord is near in the valley of decision.

—**Joel 3:14**

All of us look forward to the future. It is a good thing to have plans and dreams for tomorrow. But we can spend so much time thinking about the future that we miss out on today. God promises that when we decide to live day by day trusting in Him, we will find joy.

291. Except a corn of wheat fall into the ground and die, it abideth alone; but if it die, it bringeth forth much fruit.

—St. John 12:24

292. The seed is the word of God.

—St. Luke 8:11

293. He that receiveth seed. . . is he that heareth the word, and understandeth it; which also beareth fruit.

—St. Matthew 13:23

God says that great things grow from tiny seeds. Help plant the seed of His Word. Then just watch God's garden of believers grow and grow!

294. Straight is the gate, and narrow is the way, which leadeth unto life.

—St. Matthew 7:4

295. A highway shall be there, and a way, and it shall be called the Way of holiness.

—Isaiah 35:8

296. Though wilt show me the path of life.

—Psalm 16:11

297. Stand ye in the ways, and see, and ask for the old paths, where is the good way, and walk therein, and ye shall find rest for your souls.

—Jeremiah 6:16

Think about the highway of holiness. It is only big enough for one hiker at a time. You have to decide to walk by yourself. You can't tag along with someone else. God's highway is steep. It will require much effort to climb. Are you in shape? The highway is a very old one. There are no modern short-cuts, just the same old commandments to obey. But God promises that He Himself will be your guide. And if you follow faithfully, you will reach the place where your soul will know contentment forever. Put your feet on the path today!

298. The very hairs of your head are all numbered.

—St. Matthew 10:30

299. Cast all your cares upon him; for he careth for you.

—1 Peter 5:7

How many hairs do you think you have on your head? The average person has about 100,000. It God cares enough to count every tiny hair on your head, He surely will take care of the bigger problems.

300. I have the keys of hell and of death.

—**Revelation 1:18**

301. I will give unto thee the keys of the kingdom of heaven.

—**St. Matthew 16:19**

You know you are growing up when your parents trust you enough to give you a house key. They count on you to use it wisely, and not to lose it. God trusts us in the same way. He gives us all we need to unlock the door to Heaven. The key to His Kingdom is believing in Jesus Christ and obeying His commands.

302. For thou wilt light my candle: the Lord my God will enlighten my darkness.

—**Psalm 18:28**

303. Let your light so shine before men, that they may see your good works, and glorify your Father in heaven.

—**St. Matthew 5:16**

Were you afraid of the dark when you were little? Every shadow looked like a horrible monster until someone turned on the light. When God comes into a person's life, fears disappear. We need to be flashlights that point others to God so they, too, will no longer fear the darkness of evil.

304. God is no respecter of persons.

—**Acts 10:34**

305. But in every nation he that feareth him, and worketh righteousness, is accepted with him.

—**Acts 10:35**

Does God have favorite children, some He loves more than others? Each person who believes in Him and obeys His Word is His favorite! It doesn't matter where you come from, or whether or not your family has always loved God. He looks at your heart and says, "This is my beloved child. Come into the Kingdom, to the special place prepared just for you."

306. God setteth the solitary in families.

—Psalm 68:6

307. In the house of the righteous is much treasure.

—Proverbs 15:6

308. And she was baptized, and her household.

—Acts 10:34

They can drive you crazy, but your family is one of God's best gifts! He gives you parents, brothers, sisters, aunts, uncles, and cousins so that you will not be lonely. Often, when one person in the family comes to know God, everyone else does, too. Start serving Him together today. The things you do for the Lord will be your special family treasure.

309. A father of the fatherless
. . .is God.

—**Psalm 68:5**

310. Ye shall be my sons and daughters, saith the Lord Almighty.

—**2 Corinthians 6:18**

Not everyone has a family. Things don't always go the way they are supposed to. That's when God makes a very special promise. "I am your Father," He says. "I will be everything to you that an earthly dad would be. I will love you and watch out for you and laugh with you and comfort you. And you will know that you are my own dear child."

311. Blessed is he that shall eat bread in the kingdom of God.

—St. Luke 14:15

312. Man shall not live by bread alone, but by every word of God.

—St. Luke 4:4

313. I am the bread of life.

—St. John 6:35

314. We are all partakers of that one bread.

—1 Corinthians 10:17

Bread is the most widely eaten food in the world. It contains many of the vitamins and minerals our bodies need to stay healthy. Jesus tells us that in addition to physical bread, made from grain, we need spiritual bread, made of the things of God.

Scripture can nourish us, just as bread does. Once, Jesus was hungry and the devil tempted Him with bread. Jesus said no, and instead drew His strength from God's Word. Later in His life, Jesus gave bread to the disciples. "Whenever you eat this," He told them, "think of Me. No one who comes to Me will ever be hungry again." Then some day, we will no longer need to eat earthly bread. We will go to live with God in Heaven, and we'll eat spiritual bread all the time. What a great treat that will be!

315. For every beast of the forest is mine, and the cattle upon a thousand hills.

—Psalm 50:10

316. I know all the fowls of the mountains: and the wild beasts of the field are mine.

—Psalm 50:11

Just think of the things God knows. He knows the way the eagle's feathers knit together to form its powerful wings. He knows what the lion thinks when it pounces. He designed each leopard's spot. Beasts and cattle and creeping things and flying fowl praise Him.

317. He that believeth on me, the works that I do shall he do also.

—**St. John 14:12**

318. If ye have faith and doubt not,. . ye shall say unto this mountain, Be thou removed, and. . .it shall be done.

—**St. Matthew 21:21**

Jesus promises incredible power to those who believe in Him. Does that mean we can make miracles whenever we want to? No, God is still in charge of all miracles. But when we pray in faith and sincerely seek His will, He allows us to be part of His life-changing work. Sometimes that work is slow and quiet, and sometimes it is miraculous.

319. The secret things belong unto the Lord our God.

—**Deuteronomy 29:29**

320. But there is a God in heaven that revealeth secrets.

—**Daniel 2:28**

Many of us dream of doing great things. We want to cure cancer and stop AIDS. We want to explore Mars and discover a cheap new source of energy. We want to reverse the aging process and invent time travel and discover the secrets of the universe. The place to begin is with God. Take your questions and your dreams to Him. Then study and work hard. Keep on seeking, and the God of the universe may indeed use you to unlock one of His secrets.

321. Death is swallowed up in victory.

—**1 Corinthians 15:54**

322. He that believeth in me, though he were dead, yet shall he live.

—**St. John 11:25**

This is the promise that means the very most.

For a human being, death looks like the end of everything. The end of life, the end of hope, the end of any future. But Jesus promises that death is not the end. Those who believe in Him have to believe what they cannot see— that the dead will live again. This hope is what gives us strength when we lose

someone we love. We know, that because of Christ, we will see that person, alive and well again, in His eternal kingdom.

323. Flesh and blood cannot inherit the kingdom of God.

—1 Corinthians 15:50

324. Flesh gives birth to flesh, but the Spirit gives birth to spirit.

—St. John 3:6

The Bible tells us that we all have split personalities. One part is the earthly body, flesh and blood. Our other half is eternal, that part of our spirit and personality that will never die. Our mothers give us our physical bodies at our birth. God's Spirit comes in and gives birth to our spirit sometime later, when we invite Him into our lives. That means every believer has two birthdays. Do you?

325. A bruised reed he shall not break.
—Isaiah 42:3

326. He hath sent me to set at liberty them that are bruised.
—St. Luke 4:18

Shepherds in Bible times cut reeds and used them as whistles. After they used them for a while, the reeds would get broken and bruised. The shepherds would simply toss them out and cut new ones. God is not like this. He is so tender, He gently cares for us when we are bruised and hurting.

327. He hath put a new song in my mouth.

—Psalm 40:3

328. The Lord is my strength and song.
—**Exodus 15:2**

329. Thy statutes have been my songs.
—**Psalm 119:54**

330. In the night his song shall be with me.

—**Psalm 42:8**

Why do birds sing? Experts say there are several reasons. They sing to attract mates, to call their children or to warn of danger. But anyone who has listened to a lark's song on a bright summer day knows differently. Birds sing because they are happy.

People are like larks. When God's love fills our lives, we feel like singing. We want to sing about the benefits of obeying His law. We want to sing of His mighty power. We sing about the good new life He has given us. With the lark, we can say, "It is good to sing praises to the Lord.

331. For where two or three are gathered together in my name, there am I in
the midst of them.

—St. Matthew 18:20

332. Forsake the foolish, and live; and go in the way of understanding.

—Proverbs 9:6

When Jesus rose from the dead, He was no longer dependent on His earthly body. Through His Holy Spirit, He could be many places at once. Now He promises to be present whenever believers are together. So don't waste your time hanging around a godless crowd. Look for those who love Him. You will find His strength and power there.

333. The heavens shall vanish away like smoke.

—Isaiah 51:6

334. I saw a new heaven and a new earth: for the first time heaven and the first earth were passed away; and there was no more sea.

—Revelation 21:1

Smog, acid rain, greenhouse warming, rising oceans – pollution is destroying our environment. When Jesus returns, will there be anything left? The Bible tells us that in the last days, earth and its atmosphere will be destroyed. But God will create a new Heaven and a new earth, where He will live with His people.

335. He hath made everything beautiful in his time.

—Ecclesiastes 3:11

336. He will beautify the meek with salvation.

Psalm 149:4

Many of us do not like what we see in the mirror. We fret over freckles or pimples or wrinkles or gray hair. But God promises us a very special kind of beauty that comes from the inside. It does not depend on face creams or make-up, and it lasts forever. It is the beauty of a hear committed to Him.

337. The Lord is my fortress.

—**2 Samuel 22:2**

338. The name of the Lord is a strong tower: the righteous runneth into it and is safe.

—**Proverbs 18:10**

The American government keeps a supply of gold at Fort Knox in Kentucky. There, the walls are high and the security is tight. No one can break into Fort Knox. God is our Fort Knox. We can run to Him at any-time and know that He will keep us safe.

339. Then I will turn to the people a pure language, that they may all call upon the name of the Lord, to serve him with one consent.

—Zepheniah 3:9

340. Lo, a great multitude... of all nations, and kindreds, and people, and tongues, stood before the throne.

—Revelation 7:9

When people tried to build the tower of Babel, God scattered them to the far corners of the earth. Hundreds of different languages then developed. But God promises that at the end of time, He will restore one language to all. Then we can sing together as one people before His throne.

341. He is a buckler to all those that trust in him.

—Psalm 18:30

342. Truth shall be thy shield and buckler.

—Psalm 91:4

A Buckler is an old-fashioned word for a belt. Think how a belt helps hold your clothes together. It protects your waist and keeps your shirttail tucked in. Without a belt, everything would come undone. That's how God's truth operates in our lives.

343. He that toucheth you toucheth the apple of his eye.

—**Zechariah 2:8**

344. Keep my commandments and live; keep my law as the apple of thine eye.

—**Proverbs 7:2**

Is there something you love to see, something you look at all throughout the day? It is the apple of your eye. God looks at us that way, with eyes of love. Then He gives us His law. He teaches us to look at it and live it until it becomes our apple.

345. For with thee is the fountain of life.

—**Psalm 36:9**

346. A fountain shall come for of the house of the Lord.

—Joel 3:18

There is nothing better than a fountain of cold water on a hot summer day. We drink and drink and drink. It tastes so good! To people who are suffering from sin, the taste of God is good, too. He is our fountain of cold water, the fountain who refreshes and gives life.

347. A word fitly spoken is life apples of gold in pictures of silver.

—Proverbs 25:11

348. A word spoken in due season, how good it is!

—Proverbs 5:23

Picture this promise. Draw two big round apples. Color them gold. Then surround your picture with a beautifully carved frame of silver. It's perfect! When God controls our mouths, our words will be silver and gold, spoken at just the right time to help others.

349. Behold, I lay in Zion a foundation stone, ... a precious cornerstone.

—1 Corinthians 3:11

350. For other foundation can no man lay than that is laid, which is Jesus Christ.

A builder knows the most important part of any building is the cornerstone. It provides the strength that supports the rest of the wall. Jesus is our cornerstone. He promises that if we build our lives on Him, they will never crumble.

351. He removeth kings, and setteth up kings.

—Daniel 2:21

352. There is no power but of God: the powers that are ordained of God.

—**Romans 13:1**

Every president, every king owes his job to God.
God is the one who puts each leader in place. Some
of the leaders He chooses are good ones. Others
are evil. But each one serves for a very important
purpose, decided by God.

353. Blessed are the merciful: for they shall
obtain mercy.

—St. Matthew 5:7

354. If ye forgive men their trespasses,
your heavenly Father will also forgive
you.

—St. Matthew 6:14

355. But if ye forgive not men their
trespasses, neither will your Father forgive your trespasses.

—St. Matthew 6:15

Trespasses are sins. If we will forgive others when they sin against us, God promises that He will forgive when we sin against Him.

356. The Lord make his face shine upon thee.

—**Numbers 6:25**

357. The skin of Moses' face shone.

—**Exodus 34:35**

God called Moses to come up on Mount Sinai and spent time with Him. While Moses was there, God gave him the Ten Commandments. After forty days with God, Moses went down from the mountain. His face shone with an incredible light, because he had been in the presence of the Lord. God's presence will show on our faces as well when we spend time with Him.

358. I will restore health unto thee, and I will heal thee of thy wounds, saith the Lord.

—**Jeremiah 30:17**

359. O Lord my God, I cried unto thee, and thou hast healed me.

—**Psalm 30:2**

Jesus if the Great Physician. All healing, spiritual and physical, comes from Him. He can work through doctors and medicines; He can heal with only the power of His Word. He cares very much about our health, and does not want us to suffer. But sometimes He leaves a disease in place. We

pray and pray, but are not healed. This is when we must trust Him the most. We do not understand, but we know that He loves us and has a purpose for our disease.

360. And many other signs truly did Jesus in the presence of his disciples, which are not written in this book.

—St. John 20:30

361. But these are written, that ye might believe that Jesus is the Christ, the son of God.

—St. John 20:31

There is so much more we would like to know about Jesus. What color were his eyes? Did he understand who he was as a boy? Why did He never get married? What other miracles did He do? But the Bible promises that we have what we need. We have enough information about Jesus to decide, each of us, if He is indeed the Son of God and the Savior of the world.

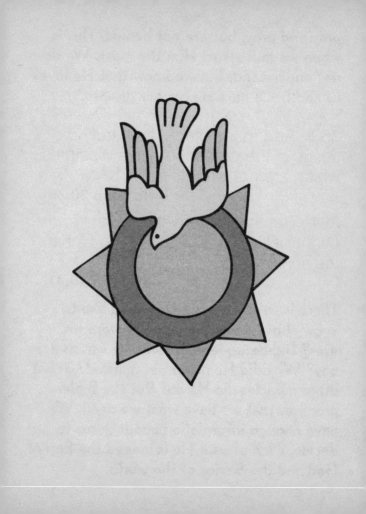

362. Call the Sabbath a delight, ...and honor the Lord.

—Isaiah 58:13

363. Then shalt thou delight thyself in the Lord; and I will cause thee to ride upon the high places of the earth.

—Isaiah 58:14

Sunday can be a long boring day. But God makes a special promise about His Special day. "Make it a delight, he says." "Enjoy worshipping in My house, and I will honor you. Spend time with me, then I will lift you high!"How will you honor God this Sunday?

364. Whereby are given unto us exceeding great and precious promises.

—2 Peter 1:4

365. That by these ye might be partakers of the divine nature.

—2 Peter 1:4

Many little boys want to grow up to be just like their dads. As believers, we feel that way about out Heavenly Father. That is why God gives us His promises. They save us from sin and make us more like Him. How great and precious His promises are!

Look for all the titles in this series

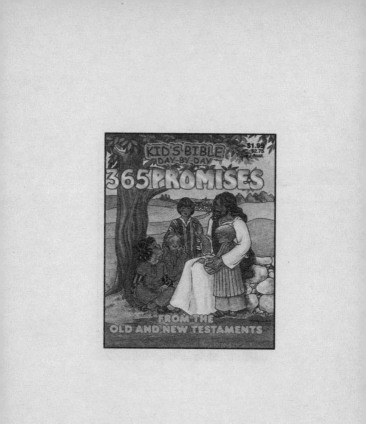